What was it like to live in
Why did the Stamp Act ma
so angry? What happened at the Boston
Tea Party? Who were the Minutemen?

Find out the answers to these questions
and more in . . .

Magic Tree House® Research Guide
AMERICAN REVOLUTION

A nonfiction companion to
Revolutionary War on Wednesday

It's Jack and Annie's very own guide to one
of American history's most important events!
Including:
- Life in the colonies
- Paul Revere's ride
- Weapons and battles
- The Declaration of Independence

And much more!

Here's what people are saying
about the Magic Tree House®
Research Guides:

Your Research Guides are a great addition to the Magic Tree House series! I have used Rain Forests *and* Space *as "read-alouds" during science units. Thank you!*
—Cheryl M., teacher

My eight-year-old son thinks your books are great—and I agree. I wish my high school students had read the Research Guides when they were his age.—John F., parent and teacher

My son loves the Research Guides. He has even asked for a notebook, which he takes with him to the museum for his research.
—A parent

I love your books. I have a great library at home filled with your books and Research Guides. The [Knights and Castles] *Research Guide really helped me do a report on castles and knights!*—A young reader

Magic Tree House®
Research Guide

AMERICAN REVOLUTION

A nonfiction companion to
Revolutionary War on Wednesday

by Mary Pope Osborne
and Natalie Pope Boyce

illustrated by Sal Murdocca

A STEPPING STONE BOOK™
Random House 🏠 New York

www.randomhouse.com/magictreehouse

Library of Congress Cataloging-in-Publication Data
Osborne, Mary Pope.
American revolution : a nonfiction companion to Revolutionary War
on Wednesday / by Mary Pope Osborne and Natalie Pope Boyce ;
illustrated by Sal Murdocca. — 1st ed.
p. cm. — (Magic tree house research guide) "A stepping stone book."
SUMMARY: Presents a picture of life in colonial America and reviews
the causes and major events of the American Revolution.
ISBN 0-375-82379-4 (trade) — ISBN 0-375-92379-9 (lib. bdg.)
1. United States—History—Revolution, 1775–1783—Juvenile literature.
[1. United States—History—Revolution, 1775–1783. 2. United States—
History—Colonial period, ca. 1600–1775. 3. United States—Social
conditions—To 1865.] I. Boyce, Natalie Pope. II. Murdocca, Sal, ill.
III. Osborne, Mary Pope. Revolutionary War on Wednesday. IV. Title.
V. Series.
E208.O83 2004   973.3—dc21   2003002179

Printed in the United States of America   First Edition
20 19 18 17 16 15 14 13 12

For Irby Pope III

Historical Consultant:

DR. CAROL BERKIN, Professor of History, Baruch College, City University of New York.

Education Consultant:

HEIDI JOHNSON, Lowell Junior High School, Bisbee, Arizona.

Very special thanks to Paul Coughlin for his wonderful photographs and, as always, to the great team at Random House: Joanne Yates, Melanie Chang, Angela Roberts, Mallory Loehr, and, of course, our editor, Shana Corey, whose skill and patience always win the day.

AMERICAN REVOLUTION

Contents

Dear Readers,

Our adventures in <u>Revolutionary War</u> <u>on Wednesday</u> were so exciting, we wanted to know everything about the American Revolution. So we decided to do some research.

First, we tried the library. The librarians helped us find books and videos. The books had great pictures. They helped us imagine how America looked in the 1700s. Then we sat down at the computer. The Internet had a lot of great sites. We read more about life during colonial times. We found out how the war started. And we

also learned how hard it was for the colonists to win. But what really impressed us the most were the people who fought for independence. They were true heroes!

So pack your backpacks and follow George Washington's soldiers. We're off to fight the Revolutionary War!

Jack

Annie

1

The Colonies

In the 1700s, our country was not called the United States. Instead of states, America was divided into 13 *colonies* (KOLL-uh-neez). A colony is land that is owned by another country.

Britain controlled the American colonies. Its king, George III, and the British government ruled them.

People often sailed from Europe and Britain to begin new lives in the colonies.

People who live in colonies are called <u>colonists</u>.

Some came for freedom to worship as they pleased. Others came for land. Still others came for work.

The trip was long and dangerous. It could take two months or more. Storms often pounded the small ships. Sometimes there wasn't enough food on board. Many people became sick and died.

Rich colonists often sent their sons to school in England.

The Colonists

In the 1700s, there were almost two million people in the colonies. Many families came from Britain. They did not think of themselves as "Americans."

Welcome to the Colonies

They thought of themselves as British. Their loyalty was to the king.

Other colonists came from Germany, France, Holland, Sweden, and Finland. Many of them came to farm the fertile land in the middle colonies. They didn't think of themselves as Americans, either. They called themselves New Yorkers, Virginians, or other names based on their colonies.

The colonies also had slaves, who were brought over from West Africa. Most slaves lived on large farms called *plantations* (plan-TAY-shunz) in the southern colonies. They worked in the fields or as house servants.

There were also American Indians in the colonies. They were there long before the colonists arrived. Many lost their lands as the colonies grew larger.

Prosper means "to be successful."

Natural resources are useful things that are found in nature.

The Colonies Prosper

By 1750, the colonies were prospering. America was rich in natural resources.

Vast forests covered the land. There was wood for building and heating houses. There was plenty of wildlife and fish for food and furs. Much of the soil was good for growing crops.

Natural Resources
Wood
Good soil
Wildlife
Fish

Many colonists made money by selling their products to England. They sold rice, furs, tobacco, wheat, and other things they grew or produced. The colonists also bought many products from England.

Turn the page to learn about the 13 colonies.

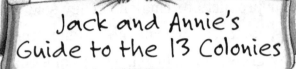

Jack and Annie's Guide to the 13 Colonies

All the colonies but Pennsylvania were on the Atlantic coast. The soil was poor in *New England*. Some people were farmers. But many New England colonists became shipbuilders, fishermen, or merchants.

In the *middle colonies*, the land was rich and fertile. Farmers grew grain that fed most of the other colonies. These colonies were known as the "bread colonies."

Tobacco was the biggest crop in the *southern colonies*. Rice was also a popular crop. Many large plantations in South Carolina grew it in the wet lowlands.

New England
Middle Colonies
Southern Colonies

Part of Mass.

New Hampshire

Massachusetts

New York

Rhode Island

Connecticut

Pennsylvania

New Jersey

Delaware

Virginia

Maryland

North Carolina

South Carolina

Georgia

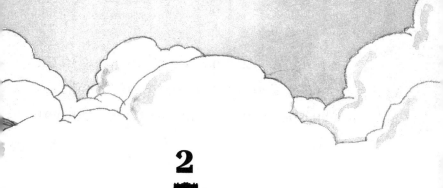

2

Life in the Colonies

There weren't many cities in colonial times. Boston, New York, Philadelphia, and Charleston were some of the largest. But compared with cities today, they were small. In 1774, Boston had only about 18,000 people. Today it has over 600,000!

Taverns were places where men gathered to eat, drink, and catch up on the news.

Colonial cities had newspapers, hospitals, and shops. There were taverns, churches, meetinghouses, and schools.

21

Livestock was often driven right through the middle of the city!

Most cities had busy harbors. At the docks, goods like rice, tobacco, and lumber piled up, waiting to be loaded onto ships.

Life on the Farms

Most people did not live in cities. Almost everyone lived on farms. Farm families worked very hard. They built their own

houses and barns. They made their own clothes, candles, and soaps. They grew much of their food. Many families worked from dawn to dusk.

Most colonists never went far from home. Travel was slow and difficult. There were no paved roads. In fact, there were very few roads at all. Most people traveled on horseback or on foot.

Nine out of every ten colonists lived in the country.

Farms were often far away from one another. Because they didn't see many people, the colonists welcomed guests. Some guests stayed for weeks at a time!

Colonial Houses

Colonial houses didn't all look alike. Some were made of brick and stone. Others were made of wood. Some were simple cabins or farmhouses. Others were beautiful mansions.

Because families were often large, children shared beds.

There were large stone fireplaces in most houses. Some fireplaces were big enough for a man to stand up in! People used fireplaces to heat their homes and for cooking.

People sat by the fire to stay warm. But even with fireplaces, houses were cold in the winter. At night, water often froze in pitchers and jugs! People warmed their beds by rubbing the covers with pans of hot coals. Except for the fire, candles gave the only light.

Windowpanes were often made of oiled paper instead of glass.

Houses had no bathrooms or running water. Almost everyone got water from wells or streams. The colonists used pots or outhouses for toilets.

 The pots people used for toilets were called "chamber pots."

Most people washed their hands and face every day. They used bowls and pitchers to wash their face and hands, but they thought bathing was unhealthy. Many colonists took a bath only once a month. And families often used the same water!

Virginia and Pennsylvania even tried to pass laws banning baths!

Food

There were few places to buy food in the country. Colonists grew vegetables in their gardens. They hunted wild game, like turkey or deer, for meat. They fished and searched for wild berries and honey.

There were no refrigerators. Colonists kept food cool in cellars.

Families cooked in pots hung over the fireplace. People ate lots of stews. For dessert they sometimes ate puddings made of cornmeal.

Jack and Annie's Hasty Pudding

1. Ask a grown-up to boil a big pot of water.
2. Slowly pour in some cornmeal. Cook for about an hour.
3. Stir it a lot with your "mush stick."
4. Pour it in a bowl and make a hole with the stick.
5. Pour some molasses, brown sugar, or maple syrup in the hole.

Education

There were not many schools in the colonies. Most children studied only a few years. Sometimes young children studied in schools called "dame schools." These schools were in a woman's home.

Girls often didn't go to school at all.

Students read from hornbooks, like this one. The page was covered with clear horn to protect it.

The quill was a hollow feather that soaked up the ink.

Many children went to one-room schools. All the grades studied together. Students wrote with goose quills dipped in ink.

Tricorn hat

Waistcoat

Breeches

Coifs

Cloak

Muff

Apron

Colonial Dress

Parents often treated children like small adults. Children even dressed like grown-ups. Boys wore breeches, stockings, and waistcoats. Girls wore long gowns and linen caps called "coifs" (KOYFS).

Many families had ten or more children!

An apprentice learns a job by working with a skilled craftsman.

Children at Work

Many children were expected to work as hard as adults. When they were six years old, some were considered full-time workers!

In the country, boys worked with their fathers. They helped build houses, tend livestock, chop wood, and hunt.

Many boys went to work as *apprentices* (uh-PREN-tus-iz). They often worked for seven years before they learned their craft.

In many homes, girls worked with their mothers. They learned to cook, sew, and make candles and soap. They also learned to spin wool and flax into cloth called "homespun." Many girls married and kept house when they were still teenagers.

Girls practiced their stitches by making samplers.

Colonists at Work

If you were a colonist, these are some jobs you might do.

<u>Teachers</u> taught school, but sometimes they also had to help churches by digging graves!

<u>Barbers</u> cut hair and sometimes worked as doctors and dentists!

LIVERY

Barber

<u>Blacksmiths</u> made things out of iron, such as shoes for horses.

Shipbuilders were good carpenters who built ships.

Printers printed newspapers, books, and pamphlets.

1742

PRINTER

Tanners turned animal skins into leather.

3

Trouble Begins

Life in the colonies was not always peaceful. For many years, the British, the French, and American Indians fought over land in North America. These battles were called the French and Indian Wars.

The conflict was long. It cost the British a lot of money. The British *Parliament* (PAR-luh-munt), or government, decided to *tax* the American colonies. A tax is what people must pay the government.

Parliament comes from the French word <u>parler</u>, meaning "to speak."

Parliament

The colonists had no say, or *representation* (reh-prih-zen-TAY-shun), in Parliament. They could not vote on these new taxes. They thought this was unfair. They complained about "taxation without representation."

The Stamp Act

In 1765, Britain ordered the colonies to pay a new tax. Everyone had to buy a tax stamp to put on their important papers. Newspapers had to be printed on special stamped paper that cost extra money. There was even a tax on playing cards!

Tax on a newspaper cost as much as a British soldier made in a day.

Many of the colonists were outraged. Throughout the colonies, men formed

These are some of the stamps required by the Stamp Act.

groups called the Sons of Liberty. These groups met in secret. They vowed to fight the Stamp Act.

On the day the tax took effect, shops were closed. Church bells rang. In Portsmouth, New Hampshire, a coffin with the word *liberty* on it was carried through the streets.

Liberty comes from the Latin word <u>libre</u>, which means "free."

The colonists even protested with teapots.

Some colonists refused to pay the tax or buy stamps. They ran tax collectors out of town. Stamp Act riots broke out in the big cities. In Boston, men burned the Stamp Act Office. The British decided to end the Stamp Act.

But many colonists were still angry. Some began calling themselves *patriots* (PAY-tree-uts). Patriots are people who love their country enough to fight for it. Other colonists remained loyal to Britain. They called themselves *loyalists* (LOY-uh-lists).

Patriot comes from the ancient Greek word patriotes, which means "fatherland."

The Boston Massacre

The British sent an extra 4,000 troops into Boston. The colonists in Boston did not want the soldiers in their city.

In 1770, a mob gathered around a

A massacre is the killing of a group of people.

It was never known who yelled the order to fire.

British soldier standing guard in front of a customs house. They began to throw snowballs filled with rocks. Other British troops rushed out to rescue him. Someone in the crowd shouted, "Fire!"

Patriot Paul Revere created this engraving of the Boston Massacre.

The British were under orders not to shoot. But they panicked. They began shooting into the crowd. Five colonists were killed. The colonists called this the Boston Massacre (MASS-sih-kur).

The Boston Tea Party

Many colonists liked to drink tea. When the British placed a new tax on tea, the colonists were very angry. In November 1773, three British ships sailed into Boston Harbor. They were loaded with tea.

Coffee became popular when the colonists gave up tea.

On December 16, a large crowd gathered at the Old South Church in Boston. They met to protest the tax.

When it was dark, some men painted their faces like Mohawk Indians. They didn't want anyone to know who they

The tea they dumped would be worth about $90,000 today.

were. The men headed down to the harbor. Quickly, they slipped into rowboats and rowed out to the ships. Then they leapt aboard and dumped tons of tea into the harbor.

The British were furious with them. King George III ordered Boston Harbor

Men used tomahawks to break open containers of tea.

closed. He put tighter controls over the colonists. In June 1774, more British troops were sent to Boston.

Liberty Trees and Boycotts

Other colonies heard what was happening in Boston. They sent food and money to help. They boycotted British goods.

The colonists also flew liberty flags from trees. They called them "liberty trees." British soldiers often cut down the trees. When they did, colonists put up liberty poles instead.

Loyalists still wanted to live peacefully with Britain. But some patriots wanted to free themselves of British rule forever.

Boycott means "to stop buying products or doing business with someone."

45

You've Got Mail!

There were no telephones, TVs, or radios in the colonies. It could take months to get mail.

Newspapers: By 1775, there were around 100 newspapers in the colonies. Some came out weekly, while others were printed every day.

Town Crier: Many towns had a town crier. He walked through the streets ringing a bell. He called out the time as well as the news of the day.

Letters: Letters were sealed with hot wax. Colonial houses had no numbers. An address often described where a person lived. It might say, "Big white house next to blacksmith shop."

Post Riders: Post riders delivered the mail on horseback. Sometimes their only roads were Indian trails. They often left letters at taverns or shops. Stagecoaches and wagons also carried mail.

4

The Shot Heard Round the World

In September 1774, 56 delegates traveled to Philadelphia. They came from all the colonies except Georgia. The delegates met to discuss the troubles in Massachusetts. They called this meeting the First Continental (kon-tuh-NEN-tul) Congress.

A <u>delegate</u> is someone chosen to speak for a group.

As they talked, the delegates began to feel more united. Patrick Henry from Virginia declared, "I am not a Virginian but an American!"

The Congress wrote a letter to King George III. They told him all the unfair things Britain had done to the colonies.

Minutemen Prepare for War

Militia comes from Latin and means "military."

The colonists prepared to fight for their freedom. Each colony had men in a *militia* (muh-LIH-shuh). The militia met several times a year to train as soldiers. These men called themselves "Minutemen."

Minutemen used this name because they could be ready to fight at a minute's notice. Some even slept with their weapons!

This Minuteman statue is in
Concord, Massachusetts.

The Ride of Paul Revere

The colonists were afraid that the British would take their weapons away. In Massachusetts, Minutemen hid guns and gunpowder in the village of Concord.

Concord is 17 miles from Boston.

The night of April 18, 1775, British soldiers left Boston. They planned to go to Concord and capture the weapons. They didn't know the patriots were watching their every move.

The signal was "One if by land, two if by sea."

A colonist climbed the tower of the Old North Church. He hung two lanterns there. That was to signal that the British were on their way across the Charles River.

A silversmith named Paul Revere knew what the signal meant. He had to warn the colonists. Paul rowed across the river from Boston. He and another rider, William Dawes, leapt onto horses. They dashed off to Concord by different roads.

One story says Paul forgot his spurs. He sent his dog home with a note asking his wife to send them.

"They promised to blow my brains out if I attempted to run," Paul Revere said.

Then Paul rode through the countryside yelling, "To arms! To arms!" Sleepy patriots stumbled out of bed. They grabbed their muskets, or arms, and rushed to head off the British.

Paul and William Dawes met up again as they raced toward Concord. They were joined by a young doctor named Samuel Prescott. As the three riders approached Concord, British soldiers

stopped them. They took Paul prisoner. But William Dawes and Dr. Prescott escaped to warn the colonists.

Lexington and Concord

The British marched into Lexington. A small group of armed Minutemen waited on the village green. Shots rang out.

Eight Minutemen were killed. The

A <u>green</u> is a grassy piece of land in the middle of a village.

One militia group raced 16 miles to reach Concord.

Retreat means "to turn back."

British marched on. But by now Minutemen from nearby villages had flooded into Concord.

When the British arrived, a group of Minutemen were waiting on Concord's North Bridge. They began firing. The British were badly outnumbered. They knew they could not win. They turned back to Boston.

As the British retreated, Minutemen hid behind stone walls, trees, and bushes. They shot at the soldiers.

The British were used to fighting in straight lines. They couldn't see who was firing at them. Many British soldiers were killed or wounded before they could get back to Boston.

The first shot fired at Lexington and Concord is known as the "shot heard round the world." The American Revolution (rev-uh-LOO-shun) had begun.

Revolution means "a sudden change in government, without an election."

Weapons of the American Revolution

Colonial weapons were bulky and hard to use.

Musket: Muskets were the most common weapon in colonial times. They were six to seven feet long. They were hard to aim and often missed. Their range was about 100 yards.

Musket

It took time to reload them between shots.

Bayonet: Muskets often had bayonets fitted on one end. A bayonet is like a sword. A musket with a bayonet on it gave soldiers two weapons in one.

Bayonet

Rifle: Rifles were about five to six feet long. A good marksman could hit objects 300 yards away with a rifle.

Rifle

Cannon: Cannons were the most powerful weapon in the war. They could hit a target several hundred yards away. The British had more cannons than the colonists.

Cannon

5

War!

Colonists from New England began gathering outside Boston. Their goal was to run the British out of the city.

On the night of June 16, 1775, a group of patriots climbed Breed's Hill. They were led by Colonel William Prescott. Breed's Hill stood across the river from Boston. They planned to build a fort on top of the hill. The men worked throughout the night.

About 10,000 patriots arrived to fight the British.

There were 2,500 British troops at the battle . . . almost twice the number of patriots.

Even though it's called the Battle of Bunker Hill, it was fought on Breed's Hill!

The next morning, the British saw that a fort had gone up overnight! Warships began shelling the fort. British soldiers crossed the river to destroy it.

The British started to climb up Breed's Hill. But their heavy weapons and packs slowed them down. "Don't fire until you see the whites of their eyes!" Colonel Prescott yelled to his men.

The patriots quietly watched and waited. When the British came closer, the colonists began to fire. They fought bravely. Twice they drove the British back. The third time, the colonists ran out of bullets. They had to use their muskets as clubs. Soon they were forced to retreat.

The battle was over. The British suffered many losses. They had won the battle. But they were trapped in Boston.

Washington in Command

In July 1775, the Continental Congress appointed George Washington to lead the colonial army.

Washington was six feet two inches tall. He was a fine athlete with a commanding presence.

Washington's army was called the Continental Army.

Washington owned a plantation in Virginia called Mount Vernon. He had fought bravely in the French and Indian Wars. People admired his strength and courage.

Washington traveled to Boston. He found a ragtag group of men waiting for him. They had come from all over the 13 colonies. Many worked as farmers, teachers, fishermen, or merchants. Most had little training for war. They didn't have uniforms. Almost all of them brought their own guns. Some brought their wives to cook and care for them. Some even brought their dogs!

British Retreat from Boston

Washington needed cannons to defeat the British. In December 1775, he asked

Boys as young as 12 signed on as cooks' helpers and drummers.

a young soldier named Henry Knox to travel to Fort Ticonderoga in northern New York. Americans had captured British cannons there. Henry's job was to haul the cannons nearly 300 miles back to Boston.

Henry began working in a bookstore when he was a young boy.

Henry and some other men left for the long journey to the north. At Fort Ticonderoga, they loaded 59 cannons onto sleds. Teams of oxen pulled the heavy loads. Snowy, rough roads lay ahead. But 56 days later, Henry and the cannons arrived in Boston!

Washington ordered his men to drag the cannons up a hill. The hill overlooked Boston.

When the British spotted the cannons, they panicked. They left Boston in March 1776.

Turn the page to check out our favorite flags of the American Revolution.

Our Favorite Flags

There was no official flag during colonial times. Many different flags flew over the colonies. Here are some of the most popular.

Grand Union Flag
George Washington used this flag in January 1776. It was the first flag of the United States.

Rattlesnake Flag
Some colonists used this flag to show they weren't afraid of the British.

George Washington's Headquarters Flag

General Washington flew this flag over his headquarters throughout the war.

First Stars and Stripes

In 1777, Congress adopted a flag with 13 stars and stripes as the flag of the United States. They represented the 13 colonies.

6

The Declaration of Independence

In May 1776, the Continental Congress met in Philadelphia. This time, the delegates came as *rebels* (REB-ulz) against the British government.

Rebel means "to fight against someone you think has unfair control over you."

There were 56 delegates from the colonies. They wanted to be independent from Britain.

The delegates decided to put this idea in a Declaration of Independence. They chose Thomas Jefferson from Virginia to write it. They asked four other men to help him. Among them were John Adams of Massachusetts and Ben Franklin of Pennsylvania.

It took Thomas Jefferson 17 days to write the Declaration. Each day he got up and played his violin. Then he put his portable desk on a table and began to write. The words he wrote would inspire

Jefferson wrote the Declaration of Independence on this portable desk.

people all over the world. And they continue to inspire us today.

Ideas in the Declaration

In the first section of the Declaration, Jefferson wrote that all men were equal. They had the right to life. They had the right of liberty and the right to seek happiness.

Second, Jefferson wrote that people should be able to choose how they want to be governed. He said that government should protect the people and respect their rights.

<u>Rights</u>
Life
Liberty
Pursuit of happiness

The Declaration of Independence said that "all men are created equal."

The Declaration also said that if the people decided their government was not protecting them, they had the right to change it. Finally, Jefferson listed all the wrongs the British had done to the colonists. He wanted everyone to know how Britain had treated the colonists.

Not fair! The Declaration did not free slaves. It did not apply to women, either. There were nearly 200 years of struggle before we had equality for all Americans.

 Fifty-six delegates signed the Declaration.

On July 4, 1776, the delegates met in Independence Hall in Philadelphia to vote on the Declaration of Independence. They voted to accept it.

The men knew that declaring independence from Britain was dangerous. If the colonists fought and didn't win, the British would punish them ... maybe even hang them.

They knew they all had to work together. Benjamin Franklin said, "We must all hang together, or most assuredly we will all hang separately."

After the vote, they rang a large bell at Independence Hall called the Liberty Bell. The bell rang all day. As the bell pealed out, people all over Philadelphia knew the Declaration had been approved.

The Liberty Bell cracked in 1846 and cannot ring today.

It was two months before all 13 colonies learned the news.

The print shops and newspapers in Philadelphia rushed to print copies for the colonists. Riders leapt on their horses and galloped away to deliver the news.

George Washington read a copy of the Declaration of Independence to the cheers of his soldiers.

Meet some stars of the Revolution.

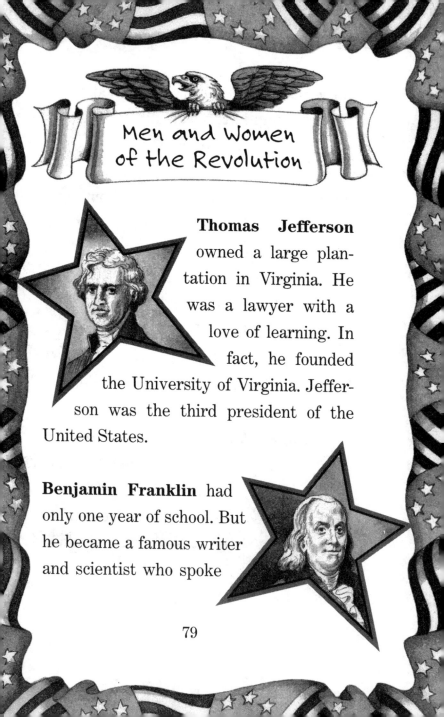

Men and Women of the Revolution

Thomas Jefferson owned a large plantation in Virginia. He was a lawyer with a love of learning. In fact, he founded the University of Virginia. Jefferson was the third president of the United States.

Benjamin Franklin had only one year of school. But he became a famous writer and scientist who spoke three languages! Franklin worked to get France's help in the war. Later, he helped write a truce with the British.

John Adams was a lawyer from New England. He believed in justice. Even though he was a patriot, he defended British soldiers accused of killing people during the Boston Massacre. He was our second president.

Abigail Adams ran the family farm alone when her husband, John, was away. She told John Adams to "remember the ladies" when making new laws for the nation.

Thomas Paine inspired the patriots by writing a popular pamphlet called *Common Sense*. In it he urged the colonists to break away from Britain.

George Washington thought he was leaving home for one year to fight the British. The war lasted eight years! Afterward, he became the first president of the United States. Our capital—Washington, D.C.—is named after him.

John Hancock was the first to sign the Declaration. He wrote his name in big letters. He did this so the king could read it without his glasses. Today, when people sign their names on a letter, they say they're putting their "John Hancock" on it.

Phillis Wheatley began life in America as a slave. Later, she was given her freedom. Phillis became a poet. Important people, including Benjamin Franklin, admired her work. She sent a poem to George Washington praising him and the Revolution.

Nathan Hale was a soldier for the Revolution. His job was to spy on the British. Nathan was caught and hanged. Before he died, he declared,

"I regret that I have but one life to lose for my country."

Patrick Henry gave stirring speeches urging revolution. In one famous speech, he said, "As for me, give me liberty or give me death!"

Mary Katherine Goddard ran a newspaper in Baltimore. In January 1777, she published the Declaration of Independence. For the first time, all the signers were listed. Later, she became the first woman postmaster in America.

7

War in the Northeast

The British did not want to give the colonies their freedom. They hired Hessian (HESH-un) soldiers from Germany to fight the patriots. The British had more men and supplies than the colonists. But the colonists were fighting for a cause they believed in. They were also fighting in a land they knew well.

Hessian soldiers were from a part of Germany called Hesse.

In August 1776, Washington and his soldiers met the British on Long Island, in what is now Brooklyn, New York. A battle began.

The patriots fought hard, but they were surrounded. A violent rainstorm began. Washington had to save his men! He asked nearby colonists to lend him their boats. In the fog, he loaded his men, horses, and cannons into the small boats. They crossed the East River to Manhattan. Then they marched north to safety.

Because of this escape, the British called Washington the "Wily Old Fox."

Crossing the Delaware

During the winter of 1776, the British and Hessians relaxed. They thought Washington's army was too weak to fight in the cold. They were in for a surprise!

On a freezing Christmas Eve in 1776, Washington had a daring plan. He wanted to attack Hessian soldiers in Trenton, New Jersey.

There were 1,500 Hessian soldiers.

Washington ordered his men to cross the Delaware River. He watched as soldiers loaded into rowboats.

Huge blocks of ice floated in the water. Rain and sleet pelted down. The tiny boats struggled through the water. Time after time, they returned to pick up men and cannons.

The Battle of Trenton

The men reached the New Jersey shore about three o'clock in the morning. They were wet and freezing. Their musket powder was damp.

The tired soldiers marched nine miles to Trenton. Some walked with their shoes falling to pieces. Their bare feet made bloody prints in the snow.

The Hessians had been celebrating Christmas. Many were drunk or asleep.

"If wet powder is a problem, we shall use our bayonets," Washington said.

The attack was a complete surprise. The Americans swooped down on the sleeping Hessians. They captured over 1,000 men. It was a big victory for the colonists.

A Victory at Saratoga

In the fall of 1777, the colonists fought British troops in Saratoga, New York. Generals Horatio Gates and Benedict Arnold led the patriots. After a fierce battle, the British surrendered.

Benedict Arnold

After the victory at Saratoga, other countries knew the colonists had a chance. The French sent ships and soldiers. Their aid gave the colonists courage to keep fighting.

Benedict Arnold later became a traitor and joined the British.

89

Molly Pitcher

Soldiers often needed help during battles. Women on the battlefield brought pitchers of cool water for the thirsty men. They also helped to tend to the wounded. These women were often called "Molly Pitcher." The women got their nickname from Mary Ludwig Hays. Her nickname was "Molly."

Molly followed her husband into battle. She helped care for the soldiers. In a battle at Monmouth, New Jersey, her husband came down with heat stroke. He could not fire his cannon. Molly stepped in to help him.

General Washington called her "Sergeant Molly." Molly died many years after the war. To honor her, a flag, a cannon, and a monument were put by her grave.

8
Valley Forge

Washington and his army spent the winter of 1777–1778 camped near Philadelphia at Valley Forge.

Congress had little money for the war. It was slow to send supplies to the soldiers. Many soldiers were wrapped in rags. Some went barefoot. Lice infested their hair and clothes.

"What is to become of the army this winter?" Washington asked Congress.

Hands and feet turned black from frostbite. Everyone suffered from the cold.

Washington later moved to a nearby farmhouse, where his wife, Martha, joined him.

Washington ordered the men to cut down trees for cabins. Until they were built, he slept in a freezing tent, just like his men.

To add to their problems, there was almost nothing to eat. Bread made of flour and water was often the only available food.

Smallpox, typhus, and other diseases broke out. Around 2,500 soldiers died from disease, lack of food, and the cold.

About 500 horses died as well.

It was the low point of the war. In February, Congress managed to send supplies. Life began to look up for the soldiers at Valley Forge.

Turn the page to meet two men who helped at Valley Forge.

Washington's Wonderful Friends

Baron von Steuben

Baron Friedrich Wilhelm Augustus von Steuben was a Prussian army officer. He spent the winter training the Continental Army. He taught the soldiers to fight in an organized way. Each day, he drilled the men on how to march and how to load their weapons. Von Steuben even wrote a training guide for the troops.

Marquis de Lafayette

The marquis was from a rich French family. Lafayette loved the colonists' idea of liberty. He came to America when he was 20.

Lafayette served on George Washington's staff and spent the winter at Valley Forge. In 1779, Lafayette returned to France. He urged the French to send more aid to the colonies. When he left America, he took some dirt with him. He loved the United States so much, he wanted to be buried in American soil.

9

End of the War

While Washington was busy fighting in the Northeast, the British were taking over the South. In 1778, British troops captured Savannah, Georgia. A few weeks later, they took Augusta, Georgia. Charleston, South Carolina, also fell to the British. By the summer of 1780, the British held much of the South.

In South Carolina, Francis Marion organized a militia. The men called

Francis Marion was called the "Swamp Fox."

themselves "Marion's Brigade" (brih-GADE). Marion and his men were fearless. They attacked without warning. Then they slipped away into the swamps. Marion's Brigade helped clear the British out of South Carolina.

George Washington sent soldiers to help the patriots. Slowly, luck turned in the South. The colonists began to defeat the British.

British Retreat to Yorktown

Cornwallis had helped defeat Washington in New York.

In March 1781, the British suffered a big loss in North Carolina. This was at the Battle of Guilford Courthouse. General Cornwallis commanded the British soldiers.

After this defeat, Cornwallis and his men retreated north to Yorktown, Virginia.

Battle of Yorktown

In August 1781, Washington and his soldiers marched to Yorktown. There, they joined French troops who had come to help.

On his way to Yorktown, Washington visited Mount Vernon . . . for the first time in six years!

The American troops greatly outnumbered the British troops. Cornwallis expected British ships to sail up the York River, bringing more soldiers to help. This did not happen.

The Americans fought their way toward the British. When they got close enough, they shelled them with cannonfire.

When Washington spotted the French ships, he jumped up and down and waved his hat.

Meanwhile, French ships arrived to help the patriots. They cut off any possibility of a British escape by water. The British had fought their final battle of the war.

101

The British Give Up

On October 17, 1781, a drummer boy marched out from the British side. He beat a signal on his drum. A British officer walked beside him. He waved a white handkerchief. Everyone knew this was a sign of surrender. One by one, the guns fell silent.

Washington accepted the British surrender. Two days later, British soldiers laid down their muskets before the Americans.

Then the French and the Americans formed opposite lines. The lines stretched a mile long. George Washington sat on his horse at the head of his men.

Half the British army in America had been captured or killed.

The British band played an old army tune called "The World Turned Upside Down."

As the British army band played, their soldiers marched off the battlefield. The fighting was finally over.

Washington's Farewell

Peace talks began in Paris. They lasted two years. In September 1783, the Treaty of Paris ended the American Revolution.

Benjamin Franklin and John Adams helped write the treaty.

In December, George Washington gathered his officers to say farewell. He walked around the room shaking hands and embracing his men. As Washington did this, he began to weep. Soon all the men were weeping with him. They had been through terrible times together. At last, their dream of a free country had come true.

Then Washington rode away to his

beloved home, Mount Vernon. He arrived on Christmas Eve. He didn't know he would soon have to leave his home again . . . this time to serve as the first president of the United States.

Washington's white horse, Nelson, carried him throughout the war.

Colonists celebrate the victory.

The Importance of the War

Everyone was overjoyed that the war was over. But America still had a very long road ahead. A new country needed to be created ... a country with freedom and justice for all.

The patriots of the American Revolution suffered great hardships for their liberty. Many left their families for years. Many risked death, disease, and freezing weather. But they did not give up.

They remain our heroes even today. Their struggles taught us that ordinary people can do amazing things. And these things can change the world.

Timeline

1689–1763 French and Indian Wars

1765 Stamp Act

1770 Boston Massacre

1773 Boston Tea Party

1775 Lexington and Concord
(The Shot Heard Round the World)

Battle of Bunker Hill

Washington Takes
Command

Doing More Research

There's a lot more you can learn about the colonies and the American Revolution. The fun of research is seeing how many different sources you can explore.

Books

Most libraries and bookstores have lots of books about the American Revolution.

Here are some things to remember when you're using books for research:

1. You don't have to read the whole book. Check the table of contents and the index to find the topics you're interested in.

2. Write down the name of the book.

When you take notes, make sure you write down the name of the book in your notebook so you can find it again.

3. Never copy exactly from a book.

When you learn something new from a book, put it in your own words.

4. Make sure the book is <u>nonfiction</u>.

Some books tell make-believe stories about the American Revolution. Make-believe stories are called *fiction*. They're fun to read, but not good for research.

Research books have real facts and tell true stories. They are called *nonfiction*. A librarian or teacher can help you make sure the books you use for research are nonfiction.

Here are some good nonfiction books about the American Revolution:

- *American Revolution*, Eyewitness Books series, by Stuart Murray

- *American Revolution: 1700–1800* by Joy Masoff

- *The American Revolution for Kids: A History with 21 Activities* by Janis Herbert

- *If You Lived at the Time of the American Revolution* by Kay Moore

- *What's the Big Idea, Ben Franklin?* by Jean Fritz

Museums

Many museums have exhibits about the American Revolution. You can also visit some Revolutionary War battlegrounds! These places can help you learn more about colonial life and the American Revolution.

When you go to a museum, historical home, or battleground:

1. Be sure to take your notebook!
Write down anything that catches your interest. Draw pictures, too!

2. Ask questions.
There are always people at a museum who can help you find what you are looking for.

3. Check the museum calendar.
Many museums have special events and activities just for kids!

Here are some museums, historical homes, and battlegrounds around the country with exhibits about the colonies and the American Revolution:

- Fraunces Tavern Museum
  New York, New York

- George Washington's Mount Vernon
  Mount Vernon, Virginia

- Guilford Courthouse National
  Military Park
  Greensboro, North Carolina

- Independence National Historical Park
  Philadelphia, Pennsylvania

- Monticello: The Home of Thomas
  Jefferson
  Charlottesville, Virginia

- Yorktown Victory Center
  Yorktown, Virginia

Videos

There are some great nonfiction videos about the American Revolution. As with books, make sure the videos you watch for research are nonfiction!

Check your library or video store for these and other nonfiction videos about the American Revolution:

- *American Colonies/American Revolution* (History Video series) from Howard Egger-Bovet, Find the Fun Productions

- *American Independence* (American History for Children series) from Schlessinger Media Company

- *Animated Hero Classics: American History Collection* from Schlessinger Media Company

The Internet

Many Web sites have lots of facts about the colonies and the American Revolution. Some also have games and activities that can help make learning about the American Revolution even more fun.

Ask your teacher or your parents to help you find more Web sites like these:

- www.42explore2.com/revolt.htm
- www.cvesd.k12.ca.us/finney/paulvm/h2_real.html
- www.mountvernon.org
- www.museum.upenn.edu
- www.pbs.org/liberty
- www.ushistory.org/betsy/flagtale.html

CD-ROMs

CD-ROMs often mix facts with fun activities.

Here are some fun CD-ROMs that will help you learn more about the American Revolution:

- *American Revolution: The Journey Toward Independence* (CD-ROM and book) by Steven Traugh from Creative Teaching Press

- *Liberty's Kids* from The Learning Company

Good luck!

Index

Photos courtesy of:

Magic Tree House® Books

Other books by Mary Pope Osborne:

Picture books:

The Brave Little Seamstress

Happy Birthday, America

Kate and the Beanstalk

Mo and His Friends

Moonhorse

New York's Bravest

Rocking Horse Christmas

First chapter books:

The *Magic Tree House®* series

For middle-grade readers:

Adaline Falling Star

After the Rain

American Tall Tales

The Deadly Power of Medusa by Mary Pope Osborne
    and Will Osborne

Favorite Greek Myths

Favorite Medieval Tales

Favorite Norse Myths

Jason and the Argonauts by Mary Pope Osborne
    and Will Osborne

The Life of Jesus in Masterpieces of Art

Mary Pope Osborne's Tales from <u>The Odyssey</u> series

Mermaid Tales from Around the World

My Brother's Keeper

My Secret War

One World, Many Religions

Spider Kane and the Mystery Under the May-Apple (#1)

Spider Kane and the Mystery at Jumbo Nightcrawler's (#2)

Standing in the Light

A Time to Dance by Will Osborne and
    Mary Pope Osborne

For young-adult readers:

Haunted Waters

MARY POPE OSBORNE and NATALIE POPE BOYCE are sisters who grew up on army posts all over the world. Today, Mary lives in New York City and Connecticut. Natalie makes her home nearby in the Berkshire Hills of Massachusetts. Mary is the author of over 50 books for children. She and Natalie are currently working together on *The Random House Book of Bible Stories* and on more Magic Tree House Research Guides.

Here's what Natalie and Mary have to say about working on *American Revolution:* "When we were children, we once lived near Yorktown, Virginia. This was where the last great battle of the American Revolution took place. We learned about George Washington and the brave men who fought there. We even played near the James River, where Washington stood to welcome French ships as they arrived to help. Later, we visited the homes of Washington and Jefferson. Their houses told us so much about these great men and how they lived. Reading, research, and visiting historic places make learning such fun, it's not even work! History comes alive right before your eyes!"